INDIANA

HELLO
U.S.A.

by Gwenyth Swain

Lerner Publications Company

You'll find this picture of oolitic limestone at the beginning of each chapter in this book. The town of Oolitic, Indiana, known as the Limestone Capital of the World, is named after this type of limestone. Oolitic limestone gets its name from the Greek words for "egg" and "stone," since it is composed of tiny granules that look like eggs.

Cover (left): Wild mustard grows on an Amish farm near Bremen. Cover (right): The Indianapolis 500 automobile race takes place every year at the Indianapolis Motor Speedway. Pages 2–3: Downtown Indianapolis. Page 3: A plow on an Amish farm near Nappanee.

This book is available in two editions:
Library binding by Lerner Publications Company, a division of Lerner Publishing Group
Soft cover by First Avenue Editions, an imprint of Lerner Publishing Group
241 First Avenue North
Minneapolis, MN 55401 U.S.A.

Website address: www.lernerbooks.com

Library of Congress Cataloging-in-Publication Data

Swain, Gwenyth, 1961–
    Indiana / by Gwenyth Swain. (Rev. and expanded 2nd ed.)
      p.   cm. — (Hello U.S.A.)
    Includes index.
    Summary: An introduction to the land, history, people, economy, and environment of Indiana.
    ISBN: 0–8225–4081–9 (lib. bdg. : alk. paper)
    ISBN: 0–8225–0778–1 (pbk. : alk. paper)
    1. Indiana—Juvenile literature. [1. Indiana.] I. Title. II. Series.
F526.3 .S93 2002
977.2—dc21   2001006137

Manufactured in the United States of America
1 2 3 4 5 6 – JR – 07 06 05 04 03 02

CONTENTS

A lighthouse beckons ships on Lake Michigan safely to the shore of Indiana.

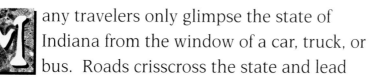

THE LAND

Crossroads of America

Many travelers only glimpse the state of Indiana from the window of a car, truck, or bus. Roads crisscross the state and lead south to Kentucky, north to Michigan, east to Ohio, and west to Illinois. Highways also give the state its motto, the Crossroads of America. But there's much more to Indiana—also nicknamed the Hoosier State—than roadways. The smallest midwestern state packs a lot of variety inside its borders.

Lake Michigan carves a half-circle of land out of northwestern Indiana. Hills along the Ohio River mark Indiana's southern boundary. Between Lake Michigan and the southern hills are farms, limestone quarries, grassy prairies, swamps, and river valleys.

Miles of interstate, city streets, and shaded paths give Indiana its motto, the Crossroads of America.

• South Bend

Hammond • Gary

Indiana Dunes National Lakeshore/
Indiana Dunes State Park

Chain O' Lakes
State Park

Fort Wayne •

Huntington •

Peru •

Portland •

• Lafayette

Attica •

Noblesville •

Mounds State Park

• Fishers

• Rockville

☆ **Indianapolis**

• Terre Haute

Beanblossom •

• Edinburgh

Nashville •

• Columbus

Bloomington •

Brown County
State Park

• Oolitic

Madison •

• Vincennes

• West Baden Springs

New Harmony •

Santa Claus •

• Evansville

The drawing of Indiana on this page is called a political map. It shows features created by people, including cities, railways, and parks. The map on the facing page is called a physical map. It shows physical features of Indiana, such as coasts, islands, mountains, rivers, and lakes. The colors represent a range of elevations, or heights above sea level (see legend box). This map also shows the geographical regions of Indiana.

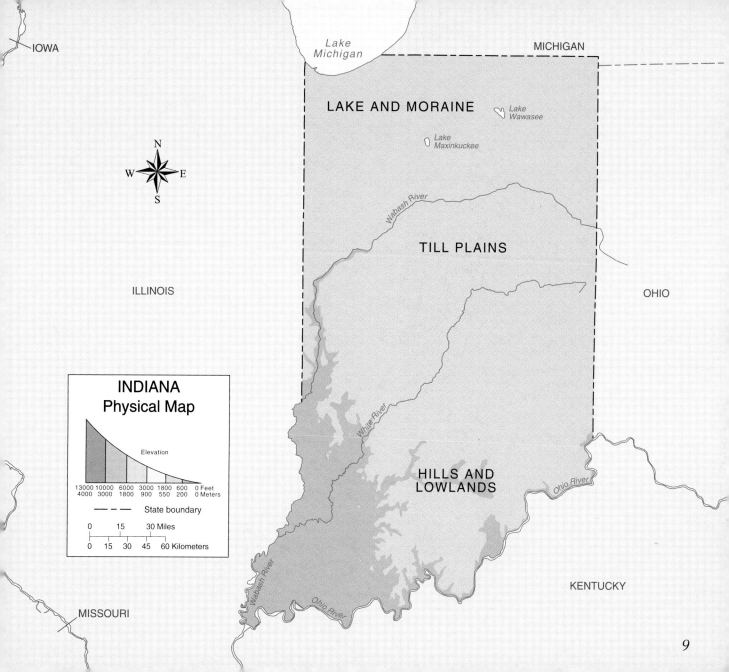

IOWA

Lake
Michigan

MICHIGAN

LAKE AND MORAINE

Lake
Wawasee

Lake
Maxinkuckee

N
W E
S

Wabash River

TILL PLAINS

ILLINOIS

OHIO

White River

INDIANA
Physical Map

Elevation

| 13000 | 10000 | 6000 | 3000 | 1800 | 600 | 0 Feet |
| 4000 | 3000 | 1800 | 900 | 550 | 200 | 0 Meters |

HILLS AND
LOWLANDS

Ohio River

- - - - State boundary

| 0 | 15 | 30 Miles |

| 0 | 15 | 30 | 45 | 60 Kilometers |

Wabash River

Ohio River

KENTUCKY

MISSOURI

9

The Ohio River
forms Indiana's
border with Kentucky.

Indiana's landscape was shaped by **glaciers,** huge sheets of ice that move slowly across land. About 400,000 years ago, glaciers pushed south from the North Pole. During the **Ice Age,** which ended about 10,000 years ago, glaciers covered the northern two-thirds of what later became Indiana.

Melting glaciers carved out many of Indiana's rivers and streams, including the Ohio, the Wabash, and the White Rivers. Indiana's longest river is the Wabash, which flows from near Fort Wayne to the state's southwestern tip.

Wherever the glaciers passed, they left behind rich soil known as **till.** In the northern third of Indiana, they wore the ground down, leaving behind flat plains and piles of sand and rock called **moraines.**

Thousands of years ago, melting glaciers formed the lakes and streams at Chain O' Lakes State Park near Fort Wayne.

Some water from melting glaciers gathered in pools to form swamps and lakes in northern Indiana. Lake Wawasee, Lake Maxinkuckee, and many other lakes dot the area. This part of the Hoosier state is known as the Lake and Moraine Region.

Rich soil and flatland on central Indiana's plains offer good farming *(above)*. Rolling hills and deep valleys run through southern Indiana *(opposite page)*.

Central Indiana, called the Till Plains region, was also once covered by glaciers, which scraped the land smooth. The region's flat plains are some of the richest in the country for farming.

The southern third of Indiana was untouched by glaciers. Because glaciers did not enrich the soil, land in this part of the state generally is not ideal for farming. Hills, steep ridges, deep valleys, and caves are common. The area's name—the Hills and Lowlands region—comes from the ups and downs of its hills and valleys.

For thousands of years after the glaciers melted, prairie grass grew in northern Indiana, while dense forests covered the rest of the state. Settlers cleared most of Indiana's trees for farming, but some forests have since grown back.

Each spring, dogwood, tulip tree (the state tree), and rosebud trees bloom. More color fills the forests each fall when leaves on oak, maple, and beech trees turn shades of yellow, red, and orange brown.

In the fall, dogwood berries brighten Indiana's forests *(above)*. A tulip tree *(right),* also called a yellow poplar, buds tuliplike flowers in the spring.

Raccoon, white-tailed deer, and skunks live in the woods of southern Indiana. Bobcats prowl the state's more remote forests.

Indiana's summers are often warm and humid, with temperatures averaging 75° F. Lots of rainfall—about 40 inches per year—and a long growing season make Indiana a good place for farming and gardening.

Winters can be cold, windy, and snowy in the north. Southern Indiana's winters are milder and sometimes very rainy. Northern Indiana receives an average of 40 inches of snow compared to southern Indiana's 10 inches. In January, Hoosiers living in Evansville often enjoy temperatures 10 degrees warmer than their northern neighbors in South Bend. Overall temperatures average 28° F in midwinter.

Perched high in a tree, a bobcat quietly watches the forest floor.

On Lake Michigan, ice sparkles near a lighthouse.

Spring flooding happens almost every year in some low-lying areas around the state. Tornadoes and severe thunderstorms are common in spring and summer. In winter, ice storms can make travel treacherous. As Hoosiers often like to say, "If you don't like the weather in Indiana, stick around. It won't be long before a change."

THE HISTORY

Becoming the Hoosier State

umans first came to what later became Indiana in about 11,000 B.C., when ice from glaciers still covered parts of the state. These people lived by hunting deer and elk.

At first people moved often, following the animals they hunted. Some of these people, known as Woodland Indians, began building villages about 2,000 years ago. Woodland Indians buried their dead inside large, log-lined pits covered with mounds of earth. Their houses did not survive, but some of their burial places can still be seen at Mounds State Park near Madison, Indiana.

More than 1,000 years ago, Mississippian Indians moved north into the area of Indiana. These Indians used wood and clay to build temple mounds shaped like pyramids. The people farmed, fished in nearby rivers, and hunted deer and other wild animals.

At one time, 1,000 Mississippian Indians lived in Angel Mounds, a town on the Ohio River near modern-day Evansville. These people abandoned their towns about 400 years ago. Experts still don't know why the Mississippian Indians left the area.

At Angel Mounds State Historic Site, a Native American weaver demonstrates her technique.

Mississippian Indians built houses at Angel Mounds, near Evansville, 1,000 years ago. This structure is based on those buildings.

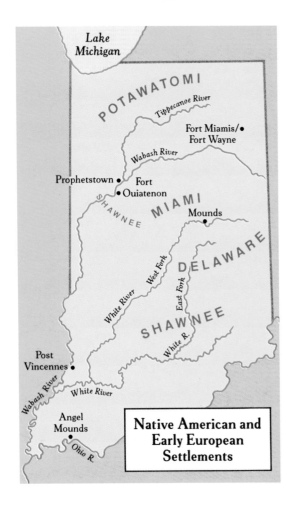

Lake Michigan

POTAWATOMI

Tippecanoe River

Fort Miamis/
Fort Wayne

Wabash River

Prophetstown •

Fort
• Ouiatenon

SHAWNEE

MIAMI

Mounds

West Fork

DELAWARE

White River

East Fork

SHAWNEE

White R.

Post
Vincennes •

Wabash River

White River

Angel
Mounds

Ohio R.

**Native American and
Early European
Settlements**

By the late 1600s, French settlers had built several forts in the Indiana area.

Miami, Potawatomi, Shawnee, and Delaware Indians moved into Indiana beginning in the late 1600s. Many had been forced from their homes in the East by wars or by European settlers.

The Potawatomi and Miami were Indiana's biggest Native American groups. They lived in small villages made up of bark-covered houses. Near their towns, they planted melons, beans, pumpkins, and corn. They also hunted deer for food and used the skins for clothing.

In the mid-1600s, French priests and fur traders may have met these Indians when they visited the Indiana area. The French explorer René-Robert Cavelier, Sieur de La Salle was the first European known to have traveled through Indiana. In 1679 Miami Indian guides led La Salle and a group of French adventurers south from Quebec. Quebec was then the capital of New France, France's empire in North America.

La Salle set up fur-trading posts along rivers and streams in the Indiana area. The Frenchmen who lived at the posts learned Indian customs, and some married Indian women. The French traded metal pots, guns, and knives for furs gathered by the Indians. France grew rich on the fur trade.

La Salle traveled through Indiana in 1679.

People in pioneer costumes welcome visitors to historic Fort Wayne, which the French originally called Fort Miamis.

Great Britain was also eager to make a fortune in the fur trade. To protect their trade and their land from the British, the French built three forts—Post Vincennes on the Wabash River, Fort Miamis at what became Fort Wayne, and Fort Ouiatenon near Lafayette. The French also made agreements with Native Americans in the area. Together, the Indians and French would fight against the British.

But forts and agreements were not enough to save France's empire. In 1754 fighting broke out between Great Britain and France. This conflict, called the French and Indian War, ended in defeat for France by 1763. Only the names of towns such as Vincennes, Terre Haute, and Lafayette remain to remind us of Indiana's French past.

After the war, the British won control of the fur trade and most of North America, including the land that later became Indiana. But the British didn't keep either for long.

Great Britain ruled several **colonies** on the eastern coast of North America. People living in the American colonies had grown tired of being governed by the British. In 1775 the American colonists began fighting a war to win their independence, or freedom.

Most battles in the American War of Independence, or Revolutionary War, were fought in the eastern colonies. But the British also planned to attack the American colonists from the western frontier, which at that time included Indiana.

Major George Rogers Clark, on the American side, thought that the best way to stop a British attack from the west was to attack the British first. In 1778 Clark captured Fort Sackville, a British fort in the old French town of Vincennes.

In 1778 George Rogers Clark led a small band of volunteers through swampland to capture a British fort at Vincennes.

Clark's expedition was one of the most important western battles in the Revolutionary War. After

several more years of fighting, the American colonists won their independence from the British. In 1783 they formed the United States of America.

By capturing settlements such as Vincennes, Clark helped the Americans claim a great deal of land that the British had controlled. Clark and his men were rewarded by the new U.S. government with land in what became Indiana Territory.

Indiana Territory was created by the United States in 1800. The territory included all of modern-day Indiana, Illinois, and Wisconsin, and the western half of Michigan. Fewer than 3,000 white settlers, most of them fur traders or former French colonists, lived in all of the territory.

William Henry Harrison was appointed governor of the new territory and arrived in the territorial capital of Vincennes in May 1800. New settlers began moving into the territory from nearby states.

Soon Indiana's settlers were ready to draft a **constitution,** the first step toward becoming a state. On December 11, 1816, Indiana became the 19th state in the Union.

During Indiana's first 30 years, Native Americans were forced to give up much of their land. Indians still living in the state found it harder and harder to survive as white settlers cleared old hunting areas. In 1830 the U.S. government wanted the land that the Indians lived on. The government began sending Indians remaining in Indiana to **reservations** in other states. Reservations were land set aside for the Indians to live on.

Potawatomi Indians lived in camps like this one at Crooked Creek. The Potawatomi were the last Native Americans to leave Indiana.

In the hot summer of 1838, the last group of Native Americans left Indiana. Nearly 900 Potawatomi were forced to march across Indiana, Illinois, and Missouri to a reservation in Kansas. So many Indians died during the journey that the Potawatomi still call this march the Trail of Death.

Tippecanoe and Tyler Too!

This catchy campaign slogan helped elect a president in 1841. What does the slogan mean?

It all goes back to 1811, when William Henry Harrison was governor of Indiana Territory. Harrison met with many Native Americans to get them to sign treaties that would take away their land. Tecumseh, a Shawnee Indian, argued that Harrison's treaties weren't legal.

Tecumseh believed that the land belonged to all Native Americans. No single Indian or Indian nation, Tecumseh said, could sell land or sign a treaty.

Tecumseh asked all Indians—even long-time enemies—to join him in saving their land. Tecumseh's followers gathered at Prophetstown, a settlement in Indiana Territory near the Tippecanoe and Wabash Rivers.

Harrison called Tecumseh a "bold, active, sensible man." But Harrison also decided that Tecumseh was dangerous.

In November 1811, while Tecumseh was away, Harrison and his troops marched toward Prophetstown. Word of Harrison's approach soon reached Indian leaders. Early on November 7, Native Americans from 14 nations attacked Harrison in the Battle of Tippecanoe. Both sides lost many men, and finally the Indians retreated. When Tecumseh returned to Prophetstown, his supporters had scattered and Harrison was claiming victory.

People remembered Harrison's role in the Battle of Tippecanoe when he ran for president in 1841. "Tippecanoe" became the former governor's nickname, while "Tyler Too" referred to John Tyler, who was Harrison's choice for vice president.

William Henry Harrison (above)

The people who in 1825 settled in New Harmony *(right)*, on the Wabash River, hoped to change the world. This progressive Indiana town became home to the nation's first preschool, first trade school, and first public library.

Abraham Lincoln spent his youth at Little Pigeon Creek *(above)* in southern Indiana.

More and more white settlers moved to Indiana after the Indians had been removed. Some settlers came because slavery was against the law in Indiana. Others came to help build canals and roads. But most of the new settlers came to Indiana to farm the land.

Thomas Lincoln and his family were typical of Indiana's settlers. Tom's young son Abraham spent most of his childhood in and around the family's log cabin on Little Pigeon Creek.

Young Abraham worked hard to help his father clear land and plant corn. There was little time left for him to go to school. During the 14 years Abraham lived in Indiana, he spent only 12 months in a classroom. Abraham lived in Indiana until he was 21 years old.

Thirty years after leaving Indiana, Abraham Lincoln was elected president of the United States. At the time, the country was deeply divided over the question of slavery. Many Southerners thought slavery was necessary. They lived on large farms, called **plantations,** and depended on African American slaves to work in the fields. Many Northerners were opposed to slavery. They thought that no person should own another person.

The two sides could not agree about slavery and other issues. By 1861, 11 Southern states left the Union and formed the Confederacy, a separate country that allowed slavery. On April 12, 1861, the Confederacy and the Union began fighting the Civil War.

In 1861 Hoosiers volunteered to fight for the Union on Civil War battlefields.

Indiana stayed in the Union, but people in the state didn't agree about slavery. Slavery was against the law in Indiana, but many settlers who had moved there from the South were not opposed to using slave labor. These Hoosiers were used to slavery. Many had slave-owning relatives and friends in the South.

Nonetheless, on the day when President Lincoln called for troops to support the Union, 10,000 Hoosiers signed up. No battles were fought in Indiana, but nearly 200,000 of the state's troops helped the Union defeat the Confederacy.

After the Civil War ended in 1865, African American slaves were freed and had the right to live wherever they wanted. Many moved to cities such

Indianapolis grew quickly after the Civil War.

In the early 1900s, these children at the Gary Public Library proudly showed off their ethnic backgrounds.

as Indianapolis to find jobs. In the late 1800s, **immigrants** (settlers from foreign countries) also came to the state to work.

Natural gas was discovered near Portland, Indiana, in 1886, and new industries began to develop. By 1906 the U.S. Steel Corporation had built a huge factory and a city, called Gary, for its workers. During the early 1900s, immigrants from eastern Europe poured into the new city. African Americans also came to work in the city's steel plants. In less than 20 years, Gary was the sixth largest city in the state, and steel was one of Indiana's most important industries.

Eugene V. Debs fought to improve working conditions for factory workers.

Steelworkers and other factory employees in the early 1900s often worked 12-hour days, seven days per week. These long hours troubled Eugene V. Debs, a young railway worker from Terre Haute, Indiana. Debs wanted to improve workers' lives. Along with shorter hours and better pay, Debs wanted workers to own the companies where they worked.

Debs helped create the Socialist Party of America to try to pass laws that would help workers. Although Debs was not always successful in achieving his goals, many of the things he fought for—such as the eight-hour workday—have since become law.

After World War I (1914–1918), Indiana's economy grew with the help of the automobile and metal industries. By the 1920s, life for most people in Indiana had become easier than it had been in pioneer times. More Hoosiers lived in cities where they could enjoy electricity and other conveniences. Many people owned cars and drove to new state parks. Hoosiers went to movie theaters and joined bicycling and hunting clubs for fun.

But many white Hoosiers worried about the African Americans who came to Indiana looking for work. Some white Indianans complained that black people and foreign immigrants were taking jobs away from them.

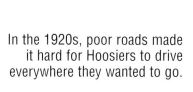

In the 1920s, poor roads made it hard for Hoosiers to drive everywhere they wanted to go.

In the 1920s, many Hoosiers joined the Ku Klux Klan *(right)*. D. C. Stephenson *(below)* led the Klan until 1925.

More than 300,000 Hoosiers joined the Ku Klux Klan in the 1920s. The Klan was a group for white people only. Members believed that white people and black people should not mix, and they sometimes used violence to support this belief.

The Indiana Klan elected a new leader, D. C. Stephenson, in 1923. Stephenson was a violent man. In 1925 he attacked a white Indianapolis woman and held her hostage. Before she died from her injuries, the woman testified against Stephenson. By the end of the 1920s, Stephenson was in jail, and Hoosiers had deserted the Klan by the thousands.

Hard times and high prices hit Indiana and the nation during the Great Depression of the 1930s. People throughout the state lost their jobs when banks failed and businesses closed. Thousands of Hoosiers left farms in the country to look for scarce factory jobs in Indiana's cities.

In the 1950s, hardworking Hoosiers helped draw new industry to Indiana.

World War II (1939–1945) boosted Indiana's economy, as demand for machinery and other factory products increased. As Indiana's economy grew stronger, more companies located in the state.

By the 1960s, Indiana was the most popular state in the nation for companies wanting to build new factories. Indiana's location—at the Crossroads of America—made it a good place to do business. Indiana's solid transportation system made it possible for companies to ship goods cheaply.

During the 1980s, many Hoosiers lost their jobs when the nationwide demand for manufactured goods decreased. Many Indiana farmers went into debt or lost their farms. The state recovered in the early 1990s with the help of new technology and new businesses.

Indiana's residents continue to make the best of their state's resources. About 91,000 miles of roads and highways crisscross the state. In 2000 Indiana enjoyed one of its best years in agriculture, ranking fourth in the United States in soybean production and fifth in corn production.

The Indiana that Abraham Lincoln knew—with log cabins and endless forests—is gone. More Hoosiers live in cities and suburbs than in small towns or on farms. Despite these changes, Indiana remembers its past and faces its future with typical Hoosier pride.

PEOPLE & ECONOMY

Hoosiers at Work and Play

ative Americans outnumbered whites when Indiana became a state, but they now make up less than 1 percent of the 6 million people living in the state. About 86 percent of all Hoosiers are white Americans of English, Scottish, Irish, and German backgrounds. Many of their ancestors left homes in Kentucky, Tennessee, and Ohio to settle in Indiana in the 1800s.

African Americans make up almost 8 percent of the state's residents. Another 4 percent of people living in Indiana are of Latino backgrounds.

Many Germans moved to Indiana in the 1800s. These Amish girls are some of their descendants.

Indianapolis is the 12th largest city in the United States.

Most people in Indiana live and work in cities and towns. Indianapolis is the state's largest city, with nearly 800,000 people. Other big cities include Fort Wayne, South Bend, Gary, Bloomington, and Evansville.

Hoosiers go to Indianapolis, the state capital, to make their opinions known to the state government *(above).* The city also offers many interesting sites for visitors *(left).*

Indiana is a major producer of prescription drugs.

More than half of Indiana's workers have service jobs, jobs in which people help others by providing some kind of service. Bank clerks, salespeople, nurses, and hotel employees are just a few of Indiana's service workers.

Service jobs in Indianapolis depend mostly on business from conventions and special events. Events such as the Indianapolis 500 Mile Race, or Indy 500, bring visitors from all over the country to stay in Indianapolis's hotels, eat at the city's restaurants, and spend money at local stores. Thousands of people in Indianapolis work to meet the needs of these visitors.

About 20 percent of all Hoosiers work in manufacturing. These workers build cars and make car parts, medicines, and steel.

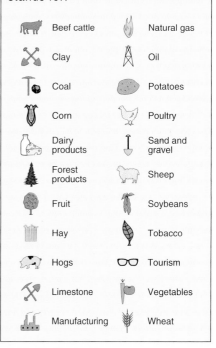

INDIANA
Economic Map

The symbols on this map show where different economic activities take place in Indiana. The legend below explains what each symbol stands for.

	Beef cattle		Natural gas
	Clay		Oil
	Coal		Potatoes
	Corn		Poultry
	Dairy products		Sand and gravel
	Forest products		Sheep
	Fruit		Soybeans
	Hay		Tobacco
	Hogs		Tourism
	Limestone		Vegetables
	Manufacturing		Wheat

A young Hoosier with hopes of being a farmer *(right)* would most likely grow corn and raise pigs *(opposite page)*. Hogs and livestock make up a large part of the state's agricultural economy.

In the 1800s, most Hoosiers farmed, but only 3 percent of modern-day Hoosiers work in agriculture. Indiana's farmers grow large crops of corn and soybeans. Many also raise hogs for bacon and pork, and chickens for their meat and eggs.

When Hoosiers aren't working, they're often playing or watching a game. Sports have long been popular in Indiana.

In 1911 drivers competed in the first Indy 500. Each May since then, thousands of fans have gathered at The Brickyard, a nickname for the Indianapolis Motor Speedway that dates back to the days when the track was made of brick.

In the first race, winner Ray Harroun careened around the track at an average speed of 75 miles per hour. At modern-day races, speeds of over 200 miles per hour are common.

Auto racing fans from across the country travel to Indiana each year to watch the Indianapolis 500.

Indiana's basketball players aren't quite as fast, but their fans pack high school and college gyms. In 1911 teams played in the state's first high school basketball tournament. Indiana's fans go so crazy over basketball that sportswriters call their behavior "Hoosier hysteria."

Fans show pride in their team at an Indiana University basketball game.

The Crispus Attucks High School Tigers

In March 1955, Hoosier hysteria swept through Crispus Attucks High School. The school—named after the first American to die in the Revolutionary War—was once the only high school for blacks in Indianapolis. The school was built in the 1920s by whites who were afraid to have their children in the same classroom with black students.

Black students did not have the same rights as whites. The Crispus Attucks basketball team wasn't allowed to play in the state basketball championship until 1942. Even then, their gym didn't have bleachers, so every game was an "away" game, held at the opposing team's gym.

Most white Hoosiers didn't think that an all-black team could win the state championship. But in 1955 the Crispus Attucks Tigers not only won, they set a new record for the most points scored in a championship game. The next year the Tigers thrilled fans again with a perfect record of 31 wins and no losses. The Crispus Attucks Tigers fought for—and won—respect on the basketball court.

In 1955 Crispus Attucks High School won the state basketball championship.

Nonprofessional sports are especially popular in Indianapolis, which is sometimes called the Amateur Sports Capital of the World. Olympic hopefuls compete at the city's swimming and track facilities. Cyclists train at the Major Taylor Velodrome.

Indianapolis has several professional teams as well. The Pacers basketball club draws fans from all over the state. Since 1984 the Colts have played football in downtown Indianapolis, first in the Hoosier Dome and later in the RCA Dome.

Football fans in Indiana gather in an indoor stadium to cheer for the Indianapolis Colts.

47

Conner Prairie
Pioneer Settlement
transports visitors
back to 1830s Indiana.

Each year Indiana's towns and cities host a variety of special events. The little town of Beanblossom welcomes bluegrass pickers for a music festival each June. History buffs can travel back in time year round at Conner Prairie Pioneer Settlement near Noblesville.

The Children's Museum of Indianapolis welcomes visitors of all ages. You can watch the world's largest water clock tell time, try hands-on science experiments, or explore ancient Egypt—and meet a 2,500-year-old mummy.

Whether you live in Indiana or are just visiting, you're bound to get a friendly welcome. Indiana is famous far and wide for its "Hoosier hospitality."

A young visitor at the Children's Museum in Indianapolis dares to get a closer look at the *Tyrannosaurus rex* display.

THE ENVIRONMENT

Protecting the Dunes

rom farm fields to forests, Indiana's greatest natural resource is its land. Since the early 1900s, Hoosiers have worked to preserve and protect that land.

In the past, protecting the land has often meant working to set it aside in parks. A unique part of Indiana's environment is preserved at Indiana Dunes State Park and National Lakeshore near Gary.

Industrial sites such as power plants *(left)* have invaded Indiana's dunes, but Hoosiers hope to keep much of the dunes intact *(opposite page).*

In the early 1900s, Indiana's dunes were leveled to make way for factories.

Bess Sheehan was just one of many Hoosiers who helped save Indiana's dunes. When she moved to Gary in 1909, the city was only a few years old. The city's houses and factories were built on flattened sand dunes along the southern shore of Lake Michigan. At first, Sheehan fought constantly against sand—sand in her shoes, sand in her food, sand in her house. But soon she was fighting to save the sand from destruction.

The sand dunes just outside the city were home to rare plants and animals not normally found in Indiana. The dunes were a special place, and Sheehan was angry that more and more dunes were being destroyed as cities and factories grew.

Bess Sheehan was not alone in her love of the dunes. She and other local women organized meetings, asked people to sign petitions, and talked to lawmakers. All their hard work paid off when the Indiana Dunes State Park opened its gates in 1926. Even more land was set aside in 1966 for the Indiana Dunes National Lakeshore.

The mayor of Gary fought to protect the dunes in the 1960s.

Indiana landfills are running out of room.

People in Indiana continue to preserve some land in parks. They also work to protect the entire state in new and different ways. The population of this smallest midwestern state has been growing steadily since the 1980s. At the same time, space in Indiana's **landfills**—holes dug in the earth for burying garbage—has been shrinking. And the number of landfills is also decreasing. In 1997 Indiana had 37 operating landfills, down from 72 in 1991.

Each Hoosier makes about one ton of solid waste, or garbage, each year. To help control this overflow, in 1990 Indiana adopted a policy that encourages people and businesses to stop throwing everything away. In 1997 the policy's goal shifted from pollution control to pollution prevention.

Recycling is easy with curbside bins.

Because of this, people and businesses in communities throughout the state are asking themselves how they can cut down on the amount of solid waste they produce. By creating less garbage, Hoosiers will turn fewer acres into landfills. The solid waste law encourages people to work together to plan how they will use and protect the land around them.

Hoosiers young and old are joining in the search for ways to stop making so much trash. They are learning the four R's—Recycle what you can, Reduce what you use, Reject products that can't be recycled, and Reuse whenever possible.

New laws and public awareness means more and more Hoosiers are recycling.

Many communities have set up ways of collecting recyclable newspaper, scrap paper, cardboard, glass, plastic, aluminum, and other items. Curbside collection points have handy, self-service bins, one for each kind of product to be recycled. From these sites, materials are trucked to larger recycling centers. The state's efforts to recycle are working. Almost 98 percent of Hoosiers have access to recycling.

Some of Indiana's companies are working to reduce waste. One company, for example, is developing a collapsible milk pouch. When the empty pouch is punched down, it takes up 70 percent less space than plastic jugs.

Milk jugs, plastic packaging, Styrofoam cups, and other throwaways take up a great deal of landfill space. More and more Hoosiers are rejecting products with too much packaging or packaging that can't be recycled. They are also reusing bags, bottles, and other containers more than ever before.

Milk pouches take up less space than cartons in a landfill.

Hoosiers are trying not to disturb too much of Indiana's natural environment. This stand of trees is preserved in Clifty Falls State Park in the southeastern part of the state.

As people make the four R's part of their lives, they ensure that Indiana's natural beauty won't be hidden under piles of solid waste. From Bess Sheehan to recycling volunteers, Hoosiers carry on a long tradition of caring for the land around them.

The Indiana dunes are a hiker's paradise.

Fun Facts

Most of the stone used to build the Empire State Building in New York City came from a hole in Indiana. In the early 1930s, the Empire Hole near Oolitic was full of limestone, a stone often used in building skyscrapers. Workers dug out enough limestone to fill a train more than 400 flatcars long. In all, 200,000 cubic feet of Indiana limestone went into making the Empire State Building.

Indiana's capital was almost named Tecumseh, after the Shawnee Indian leader who lived in Prophetstown, Indiana, in the early 1800s.

Empire Hole

No one knows the exact origin of the word "Hoosier," the nickname for people from Indiana. Poet James Whitcomb Riley has an explanation, which may or may not be true. He claimed that in pioneer times, Indiana was a rough place. After a terrible fight in a bar, one man looked on the floor. He asked, "Whose ear?" and the state's nickname was born.

The first pay toilet in the United States opened for business in 1910 at the Terre Haute, Indiana, train station.

In 1871 Fort Wayne, Indiana, hosted the first professional baseball game. The Fort Wayne Kekiongas defeated the Cleveland Forest Citys 2–0.

An Indianapolis man created Raggedy Ann in 1915. Johnny Gruelle fixed up an old, battered doll and began making up stories about the doll to entertain his daughter. Gruelle later wrote down these stories, which have been published as the Raggedy Ann Books.

STATE SONG

Indiana's state song was written in 1897 and adopted in 1913.

ON THE BANKS OF THE WABASH, FAR AWAY

Words and music by Paul Dresser

Round my In-di-an-a home-stead wave the corn-fields, In the dis-tance loom the wood-lands clear and cool. Of-ten times my thoughts re-vert to scenes of child-hood, Where I first re-ceived my les-sons, na-ture's school. Oh, the moon-light's fair to-night a-long the Wa-bash, From the fields there comes the breath of new mown hay. Thru the syc-a-mores the can-dle lights are gleam-ing On the banks of the Wa-bash, far a-way.

You can hear "On the Banks of the Wabash, Far Away" by visiting this website:
<http://www.50states.com/songs/indiana.htm>

A HOOSIER RECIPE

Corn is one of Indiana's leading agricultural products. This easy recipe uses three versions of the Hoosier State's favorite vegetable. Ask an adult for help with all steps involving an oven.

THREE-CORN CASSEROLE

You will need:

½ cup butter, softened
1 cup sour cream
1 egg

1 16-ounce can whole kernel corn, drained
1 16-ounce can cream style corn
1 9-ounce package corn muffin mix

1. Preheat oven to 375° F.
2. Mix butter, sour cream, and egg.
3. Stir in both cans of corn.
4. Add dry muffin mix and blend.
5. Spoon into a greased casserole dish.
6. Bake casserole one hour or until top is brown and crispy.

Makes 6 to 8 servings.

HISTORICAL TIMELINE

11,000 B.C.   The first humans arrive in the area that later became Indiana.

A.D. 900   Mississippian Indians begin living along the Ohio River.

1679   The French explorer René-Robert Cavelier, Sieur de La Salle travels through Indiana.

1732   The French establish the first permanent white settlement in Indiana at Post Vincennes.

1763   Britain takes control of the North American fur trade, including French posts in Indiana, after defeating France in the French and Indian War (1754–1763).

1778   George Rogers Clark's troops capture Fort Sackville.

1800   The U.S. government creates Indiana Territory.

1811   William Henry Harrison's troops defeat Native Americans at the Battle of Tippecanoe.

1816   Indiana becomes the 19th state.

1838 Potawatomi Indians in Indiana Territory are forced to a reservation in Kansas.

1861 Hoosiers side with Union troops in the Civil War (1861–1865).

1886 Natural gas is discovered at Portland, Indiana.

1906 The U.S. Steel Corporation builds steel mills in Gary.

1911 Drivers compete in the first Indianapolis 500 race.

1920 For the first time, more Hoosiers live in cities than in the country.

1926 Indiana Dunes State Park opens.

1930s Many Hoosiers leave their farms to look for jobs in Indiana's cities.

1966 Indiana Dunes National Lakeshore is created.

1988 Indiana senator J. Danforth Quayle is elected vice president of the United States.

2000 Indiana farmers harvest record crops of soybeans and corn.

OUTSTANDING HOOSIERS

Larry Bird

Hoagy Carmichael

Levi Coffin

Larry Bird (born 1956) is considered one of the finest basketball players in the game's history. Born in West Baden, Indiana, Bird attended Indiana State University in Terre Haute and was named College Basketball Player of the Year in 1979. Later that year he began playing for the Boston Celtics and helped lead the team to the World Championship in 1981, 1984, and 1986. He went on to coach the Indiana Pacers in the 1997-1998 season.

Hoagy Carmichael (1899–1981) was a musician who began writing songs as a student at Indiana University in the 1920s. His slow and haunting melodies include "Stardust" and "Georgia on My Mind." Carmichael was born in Bloomington.

Levi Coffin (1798–1877) became known as the "President of the Underground Railroad" because he helped thousands of slaves from the South travel north to freedom. Coffin moved to Fountain City, Indiana, in 1826. He owned a general store and refused to sell any goods made under the Southern slave system.

Jim Davis (born 1945), from Marion, Indiana, is a cartoonist best known as the creator of Garfield, a *very* grumpy cat who has his own cartoon strip. And from 1988 to 1994, Garfield was the star of the television cartoon *Garfield and Friends.*

James Dean (1931–1955) was a movie star who became famous for his roles as a confused, rebellious youth. Dean, who was born in Marion, Indiana, starred in the big-screen hits *Rebel without a Cause*, *Giant*, and *East of Eden.*

Jim Davis and Garfield

John Dillinger (1902–1934) was an outlaw who terrorized the Midwest during the early 1930s with daring bank robberies and prison breaks. Captured and jailed in Crown Point, Indiana, Dillinger escaped using a fake pistol carved out of wood. A few months later in Chicago, FBI agents gunned him down. Dillinger was born in Indianapolis.

John Dillinger

Virgil "Gus" Grissom (1926–1967) was the first American astronaut to explore space twice. The Mitchell, Indiana, native died during a practice run for the launching of *Apollo I*, the first mission to explore the Moon.

Richard Hatcher

Richard Hatcher (born 1933) was one of the first African Americans to serve as mayor of a large city. Mayor Hatcher was elected mayor of Gary, Indiana, in 1967. He was re-elected to the office four times.

Janet Jackson (born 1966) is one of the world's most successful recording artists. Born in Gary, Indiana, Jackson began performing as a child, opening for her famous brothers' group, the Jackson Five. As a teenager, she starred on the television series *Good Times* and *Fame.* Jackson has sold more than 40 million albums and has won three Grammy Awards. Her most popular albums include *Control* and *All for You.*

Janet Jackson

David Letterman (born 1947) is a television comedian and host of *The Late Show with David Letterman.* Born in Indianapolis, he started his career as a weatherman. Letterman once reported that hailstones "bigger than canned hams" were falling.

David Letterman

John Mellencamp

Jane Pauley

Ernie Pyle

Marshall "Major" Taylor

John Mellencamp (born 1951) was born in Seymour, Indiana. He is known for his blend of pop, rock, and country music. In songs such as "Small Town" and "Pink Houses," Mellencamp's songs tell the stories of working-class Americans living in small towns.

Jane Pauley (born 1950) is a television news reporter who grew up in Indianapolis. Her first job as a reporter was at an Indianapolis TV station. She was cohost of *The Today Show* for 13 years. Since 1992 she has been an anchor on *Dateline NBC*. Pauley has won many awards for her reporting, including an Emmy in 1997.

Cole Porter (1891–1964) was a composer who wrote many popular songs and music for Broadway shows. His most famous songs include "I Get a Kick Out of You," "I've Got You Under My Skin," and "You're the Top." Porter was born in Peru, Indiana.

Ernie Pyle (1900–1945), a newspaper reporter, was born on a farm near Dana, Indiana. Pyle covered World War II. In his articles, Pyle focused on the lives of ordinary soldiers instead of generals. He won many awards, including the 1944 Pulitzer Prize for reporting. While on assignment overseas, he was killed by enemy fire.

James Whitcomb Riley (1849–1916), born in Greenfield, Indiana, was known as "the poet of the common people." His poems, which often celebrate the sights and sounds of rural Indiana, include "When the Frost Is on the Punkin" and "The Raggedy Man."

Marshall "Major" Taylor (1878–1932) was a cyclist born in Indianapolis. Taylor, who broke several world records, was the world champion bicycle racer in 1899. Because Taylor was African American, he was not allowed to race in many American cities. Cyclists now race in Indianapolis at the Major Taylor Velodrome.

Tenskwatawa (1768?–1834), also known as the Shawnee Prophet, was a religious leader for Native Americans. Tenskwatawa moved to Prophetstown, near present-day Lafayette, in the early 1800s. With his brother Tecumseh, he brought Indians from different nations together in an alliance against white settlers.

Tenskwatawa

Twyla Tharp (born 1941) is a dancer, director, and choreographer who creates modern dances set to classical, jazz, and popular music. Tharp ran her own dance company from 1965 to 1988. She was born in Portland, Indiana.

Twyla Tharp

Kurt Vonnegut Jr. (born 1922) is a writer from Indianapolis. He has written many best-selling novels including *God Bless You, Mr. Rosewater*; *Slaughterhouse Five*; and *Cat's Cradle*. His novels often use science-fiction and fantasy.

Jessamyn West (1902–1984) wrote books based on her upbringing in Jennings County, Indiana. In *Massacre at Fall Creek*, she tells the true story of nine Indians murdered by white settlers. The settlers were put on trial in Pendleton, Indiana, in 1824. This was the first time white Americans were tried for killing Native Americans.

Jessamyn West

Ryan White (1971–1990) was an activist who suffered from hemophilia, a blood disease. White was accidentally given blood contaminated with HIV, the virus that causes AIDS. In 1985 parents in his hometown of Kokomo, Indiana, banned him from going to school with their children. White sued the school board and won his fight to go to school. His efforts helped other people overcome their fear of AIDS.

Ryan White

FACTS-AT-A-GLANCE

Nickname: The Hoosier State

Song: "On the Banks of the Wabash, Far Away"

Motto: The Crossroads of America

Flower: peony

Tree: tulip tree

Bird: cardinal

Stone: limestone

River: Wabash River

Date and ranking of statehood: December 11, 1816, the 19th state

Capital: Indianapolis

Area: 35,870 square miles

Rank in area, nationwide: 38th

Average January temperature: 28° F

Average July temperature: 75° F

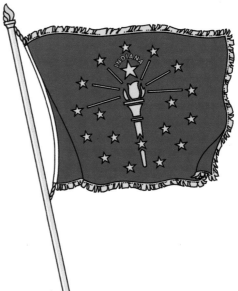

The Indiana flag features 19 stars, representing Indiana's place as the 19th state in the Union.

POPULATION GROWTH

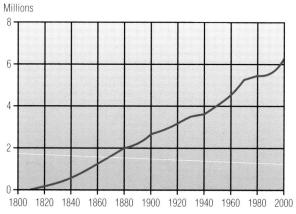

Millions

This chart shows how Indiana's population has grown from 1810 to 2000.

Population: 6,080,485 (2000 census)

Rank in population, nationwide: 14th

Major cities and populations: (2000 census) Indianapolis (791,926), Fort Wayne (205,727), Evansville (121,582), South Bend (107,789), Gary (102,746), Hammond (83,048), Bloomington (69,291)

U.S. senators: 2

U.S. representatives: 9

Electoral votes: 11

Natural resources: clay, gravel, gypsum, limestone, peat, petroleum, sand, soft coal, soil

Agricultural products: apples, beef cattle, corn, cucumbers, eggs, hay, hogs, milk, soybeans, tomatoes, wheat

Mining: gravel, gypsum, limestone, sand, soft coal, stone

Manufactured goods: airplane parts, chemicals, electrical equipment, food products, machinery, medicine, plastics, steel, transportation equipment

Between 1816 and 1963, more than 200 variations of the state seal existed. Indiana's current seal shows a pioneer scene. The setting sun represents Indiana as an important part of westward expansion.

WHERE HOOSIERS WORK

Services—59 percent (services include jobs in trade; community, social, and personal services; finance, insurance, and real estate; transportation, communication, and utilities)

Manufacturing—20 percent

Government—12 percent

Construction—6 percent

Agriculture—3 percent

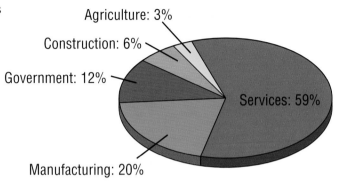

GROSS STATE PRODUCT

Services—52 percent (services include jobs in trade; community, social, and personal services; finance, insurance, and real estate; transportation, communication, and utilities)

Manufacturing—31 percent

Government—10 percent

Construction—5 percent

Agriculture—2 percent

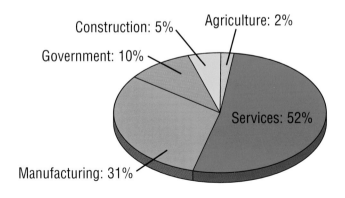

INDIANA WILDLIFE

Mammals—bobcat, deer, gray bat, Indiana bat, muskrat, opossum, rabbit, raccoon, skunk, woodchuck

Birds—barn owl, blue jay, golden-winged warbler, oriole, prairie lark, sandhill crane, wood thrush, yellow-winged sparrow

Amphibians and reptiles—bull snake, ground skink, hieroglyphic turtle, snapping turtle, spotted turtle, timber rattlesnake

Fish—bass, bluebreast darter, catfish, pickerel, pike, salmon, sunfish, Tippecanoe darter

Trees—ash, beech, black walnut, black willow, elm, hickory, maple, oak, persimmon, sycamore, yellow poplar

Wild plants—iris, jack-in-the-pulpit, nodding trillium, orchid, ox-eye daisy, peony, peppermint, pipewort, Queen Anne's lace, spearmint, sweet clover

Woodchucks, also known as groundhogs, make their homes in Indiana's forests and prairies.

PLACES TO VISIT

Angel Mounds State Historic Site, Evansville
Inhabited by Mississippian Indians from about 1100 to 1450, Angel Mounds features a preserved ancient Native American site. Visitors can explore platform mounds, nature trails, and exhibits.

Brown County State Park, near Nashville
Visitors to Indiana's largest state park can hike the trails, go fishing, or check out the nature center.

Children's Museum, Indianapolis
Indianapolis has one of the largest children's museums in the world. The museum features 10 interactive galleries, special exhibits, a planetarium, and a five-story CineDome.

Conner Prairie Pioneer Settlement, Fishers
This living-history museum has a Museum Center, an 1836 village, an interactive Pioneer Adventure Area, and more.

Grissom Air Museum, Peru
Named after astronaut and Indiana native Virgil "Gus" Grissom, the museum features a collection of vintage military aircraft and aviation memorabilia.

Holiday World & Splashin' Safari, Santa Claus
Visitors to this amusement park can ride roller coasters, splash in a water park, and watch live music shows.

Indianapolis Motor Speedway Hall of Fame Museum, Indianapolis

One of the world's largest racing exhibits, the museum features classic and antique cars, video presentations, racing memorabilia, and some of the Indianapolis 500 cars.

Indianapolis Museum of Art, Indianapolis

The museum's attractions include 152 acres of parkland, with gardens, pavilions, a theater, and greenhouses. Also on display are ancient and modern art.

Mathers Museum of World Cultures, Bloomington

Visitors to this museum can learn about objects and cultures from around the world.

NCAA Hall of Champions, Indianapolis

This complex includes four theaters and a video wall covered with more than 100 monitors. Visitors can also check out interactive displays and a gift shop.

Studebaker National Museum, South Bend

Learn more about the 114 years of Studebaker automotive history, from the pioneer wagons to the first high-performance autos.

WonderLab, Bloomington

Kids can explore the world of science with the lab's exhibits and demonstrations. Hands-on activities help young scientists learn more about the natural world.

ANNUAL EVENTS

High School Basketball Tournament, Indianapolis—*March*

Jazz in the Valley, West Baden—*March*

Dogwood Festival, Perry County—*April*

Indianapolis 500 Festival—*May*

Bill Monroe's Bluegrass Festival, Beanblossom—*June*

Scottish Festival, Columbus—*July*

Indiana State Fair, Indianapolis—*August*

Fall Festival, Edinburgh—*September*

Potawatomi Festival, Attica—*September*

Parke County Covered Bridge Festival, Rockville—*October*

Christmas at Conner Prairie, Fishers—*December*

LEARN MORE ABOUT INDIANA

BOOKS

General

Fradin, Dennis Brindell, and Judith Bloom Fradin. *Indiana*. Chicago: Children's Press, 1997.

Heinrichs, Ann. *Indiana*. Danbury, CT: Children's Press, 2000.

Special Interest

Cwiklik, Robert. *Tecumseh: Shawnee Rebel*. New York: Chelsea House, 1993. Tecumseh, a Shawnee chief, almost succeeded in creating an Indian confederacy against white settlers in the Midwest.

Dolan, Sean. *Larry Bird*. New York: Chelsea House, 1994. This biography covers the life of the basketball legend, who started his career playing on Indiana's courts.

Joseph, Paul. *William H. Harrison*. Minneapolis, MN: Abdo & Daughters, 2000. This biography describes the life of William Henry Harrison, governor of the Indiana Territory and ninth president of the United States.

Rubel, David. *How to Drive an Indy Race Car*. Santa Fe, NM: J. Muir Publications, 1992. Al Unser Jr. takes readers behind the wheel to share the science behind Indy racing.

Swain, Gwenyth. *President of the Underground Railroad: A Story about Levi Coffin*. Minneapolis, MN: Carolrhoda Books, Inc., 2001.

Fiction

Bradley, Kimberly Brubaker. *Ruthie's Gift*. New York: Delacorte Press, 1998. Set in a small town in Indiana in 1915, this book tells the story of eight-year-old Ruthie, the only girl in a family of six boys. Ruthie struggles to be herself and the "lady" her mother wants her to be.

Haddix, Margaret Peterson. *Running Out of Time*. New York: Simon and Schuster, 1995. Thirteen-year-old Jessie thinks she lives in 1840. But when her mother sends her outside their Indiana village to get help for sick children, Jessie learns that the year is really 1996. She discovers that her home is part of a experimental village built by scientists for tourists to observe. For older readers.

Sanders, Scott Russell. *The Floating House*. New York: Macmillan Books, 1995. In 1815 the McClure family sets sail down the Ohio River and settles in what would later become Indiana.

Stratton-Porter, Gene. *Laddie: A True Blue Story*. Bloomington, IN: Indiana University Press, 1988. This novel by one of Indiana's most celebrated authors tells the story of Laddie as he fights to help the woman he loves. For older readers.

Wyman, Andrea. *Red Sky at Morning*. New York: Holiday House, 1991. Left alone on the family farm in Indiana, Callie faces hardships when she must take care of her ailing grandfather.

WEBSITES

accessIndiana

<http://www.state.in.us/>

Visit the Hoosier State's official website to learn more about living and working in Indiana. The site includes history, maps, and links for more information.

Enjoy Indiana

<http://www.enjoyindiana.com/>

Learn about places to go and things to do in the Hoosier State. The site also features general information about Indiana.

Fun On-line

<http://www.childrensmuseum.org/funonline/funonline.html>

See what the Children's Museum of Indianapolis, the largest children's museum in the world, has to offer by checking out this website. The site features information and activities related to the museum's art, science, and history exhibits.

Indianapolis Star

<http://www.starnews.com/>

The online version of the state's largest newspaper covers current events and Indiana's sports teams.

PRONUNCIATION GUIDE

Hoosier (HOO-zhur)

Lafayette (law-fee-EHT)

La Salle (luh SAL)

Maxinkuckee (mak-sin-KUHK-ee)

Oiatenon (WEE-a-teh-nahn)

Oolitic (oo-LIHT-ihk)

Potawatomi (pah-tuh-WAH-tuh-mee)

Shawnee (shaw-NEE)

Tecumseh (tuh-KUHMP-suh)

Tenskwatawa (ten-SKWAH-tuh-wah)

Terre Haute (teh-ruh HOHT)

Tippecanoe (tip-ee-kuh-NOO)

Wyandotte (WY-uhn-daht)

GLOSSARY

colony: a territory ruled by a country some distance away

constitution: the system of basic laws or rules of a government, society, or organization; the document in which these laws or rules are written

glacier: a large body of ice and snow that moves slowly over land

ice age: a period when glaciers cover large regions of the earth. The term *Ice Age* usually refers to the most recent one, called the Pleistocene, which began almost 2 million years ago and ended about 10,000 years ago.

immigrant: a person who moves to a foreign country and settles there

landfill: a place specially prepared for burying solid waste

moraine: a mass of sand, gravel, and rocks pushed along or left behind by a glacier

plantation: a large estate, usually in a warm climate, on which crops are grown by workers who live on the estate. In the past, plantation owners often used slave labor.

reservation: public land set aside by the government to be used by Native Americans

till: a rich mixture of clay, sand, and gravel dragged along by a glacier and left behind when the ice melts

INDEX

PHOTO ACKNOWLEDGMENTS

Cover photographs by © Bob Rowan; Progressive Image/CORBIS (left) and © Reuters NewMedia Inc./CORBIS (right); PresentationMaps.com, pp. 1, 8, 9, 41; © Richard Cummins/CORBIS, pp. 2–3, 6; © Bob Rowan; Progressive Image/CORBIS, p. 3; © A. J. Copley/Visuals Unlimited, pp. 4, 7 (inset), 17 (inset), 37 (inset), 50 (inset); © Joseph Sohm/CORBIS, pp. 7, 38; © (1992) Daniel Dempster, pp. 10, 56, 60; Richard Fields—Indiana DNR, pp. 11, 19, 54, 80; Indiana Farm Bureau, Inc., pp. 12, 43 (bottom); © (1992) Adam Jones, pp. 13, 14 (left); © Gary W. Carter/CORBIS, p. 14 (right); Maslowski Photo, p. 15; © J. Madeley/Root Resources, p. 16; Evansville Convention & Visitors Bureau, p. 18; Indiana Historical Society Library, pp. 21 (neg. #C5188), 28 (right, neg. #C2375), 29 (neg. #C5187); © Paul L. Meyers/Root Resources, p. 22; © Culver Pictures, p. 24; Tippecanoe County Historical Association, Lafayette, Indiana, Gift of Mrs. Cable G. Ball, p. 26; Library of Congress, pp. 27, 32; National Park Service, Lincoln Boyhood National Memorial, p. 28 (left); Indiana Historical Society, pp. 30, 69 (top); Calumet Regional Archives, Indiana University Northwest, pp. 31, 52, 53; Indiana State Library, Indiana Division, pp. 34 (both), 35, 66 (second from bottom), 68 (bottom), 69 (second from bottom); © Root Resources, p. 37; © James P. Rowan, p. 39 (left); Ed Hansen, pp. 39 (right), 42, 43 (top); Eli Lilly and Company, Indianapolis, Indiana, p. 40; © Duomo/CORBIS, p. 44; Indiana University, p. 45; Photograph by *Indianapolis Recorder*/Indiana Historical Society Library, p. 46 (neg. no. C5206); © ALLSPORT USA/Matthew Stockman, p. 47; © JeffGreenberg@juno.com, p. 48 (left); Indianapolis Convention & Visitors Association, p. 48 (right); © Patrick Bennett/CORBIS, pp. 49, 50, 58; © Peter Pearson/Root Resources, p. 51; Christanne Traxler, p. 55; *Du Pont Magazine*, p. 57; © Earl L. Kubis/Root Resources, p. 59; Jack Lindstrom, p. 61; Tim Seeley, pp. 63, 71 (top), 72; © John Barrett/Globe Photos, Inc., p. 66 (top); Duncan P. Schiedt, p. 66 (second from top); Dale Wittner, p. 66 (bottom); USIA, National Archives, p. 67 (top); Office of the Mayor, Gary, Indiana, p. 67 (second from top); © Fitzroy Barrett/Globe Photos, Inc., p. 67 (second from bottom); © Globe Photos, Inc., p. 67 (bottom); Gary Gershoff/Retna Ltd., p. 68 (top); © Mitchell Levy, Rangefinder/Globe Photos, Inc., p. 68 (second from top); Army Signal Corps, National Archives, p. 68 (second from bottom); Twyla Tharp Dance Foundation, p. 69 (second from top); AP/Wide World Photos, p. 69 (bottom); Jean Matheny, p. 70 (top); © Tom Brakefield/CORBIS, p. 73.